CITIES IN MOTION

POEMS BY

SYLVIA MOSS

THE NATIONAL POETRY SERIES

SELECTED BY DEREK WALCOTT

Cities in Motion

CITIES
IN
MOTION

POEMS BY
SYLVIA MOSS

University of Illinois Press
Urbana and Chicago

Acknowledgment is made to the following publications, in which these poems first appeared: *The Grolier Poetry Prize 1986*, "Mutable Earth," "Polished Fragment"; *Helicon Nine*, "The Idea of North," "Proof"; *The New Laurel Review*, "The Daughters of Edward Boit," "Long Illness"; *New Letters*, "1913," "Steamer to Feodosiya."

"Summer Night" is the title of a landscape (*"Sommernatt,"* 1899) by the Norwegian painter Harald Sohlberg. Part IV of "The Face of the Enemy" makes free use of transcripts from the 1945 trial of Vidkun Quisling for high treason. *"Liebeslieder Walzer"* is the title of a series of waltzes by Brahms—music later used by Balanchine for a ballet of the same name. The last line of "Coffee Trees" is from a letter by Karen Blixen.

I wish to thank the Corporation of Yaddo for its support. And for criticism and friendship by turns, my gratitude to Louise Glück, Michael Ryan, and Ellen Bryant Voigt.

S. M.

This book is printed on acid-free paper.

Library of Congress Cataloging-in-Publication Data

Moss, Sylvia
    Cities in motion.

    (The National poetry series)
    I. Title. II. Series.
PS3563.08855C5 1987   811'.54   87-5003
ISBN 0-252-01436-7 (alk. paper)

The National Poetry Series

The National Poetry Series was established in 1978 to publish five collections of poetry annually through five participating publishers. The manuscripts are selected by five poets of national reputation. Publication is funded by James A. Michener, Edward J. Piszek, The Copernicus Society of America, The National Endowment for the Arts, The Friends of the National Poetry Series, and the five publishers—E. P. Dutton, Graywolf Press, William Morrow & Co., Persea Books, and The University of Illinois Press.

1986

JUNK CITY
Barbara Anderson
Selected by Robert Pinsky/Persea Books

CARDINALS IN THE ICE AGE
John Engels
Selected by Philip Levine/Graywolf Press

LITTLE STAR
Mark Halliday
Selected by Heather McHugh/William Morrow

CITIES IN MOTION
Sylvia Moss
Selected by Derek Walcott/University of Illinois Press

RED ROADS
Charlie Smith
Selected by Stanley Kunitz/E. P. Dutton

To my father and mother

Contents

I

Steamer to Feodosiya

In Chekhov's story two lovers
sit in the public gardens
watching the steamer to Feodosiya —
you are like them both,
like the man and like the woman

sitting on a bench at Yalta.
Almost evening and they do not speak.
The man is married to another woman,
the woman to another man, and the end,
the ending of their story

is so far off this evening.
The cypress ripples, the lilac water blackens,
and you are still sitting in Chekhov's story
because it is your story
and you cannot know the ending.

Mutable Earth

Because he is crying
I call my son to the window.

Andromeda, the Twins, the Ram
slide to their places
in the sudden dark. We find
Orion's belt, the blue star
that is his shoulder,

and the boy forgets he is afraid to sleep.

This is the winter sky,
chalked in, safe,
familiar as a map of Earth;
the great Hunter always
in pursuit—and after, Gemini.
Imagine twin boys, so unalike,
so avid for each other;
together they hold a harp—
one deathless, one the mortal brother.

1913

All forests lead you back
to that first forest:
fox prints that turn in circles,
the faint bells, white curls of breath
drift from your icy lips.
Your mother holds your hand.
She won't let you stop running.

A boy who never saw your face
is looking for you. In your house
someone fingers your mother's dress
and takes apart the mattress.
The floorboards catch like tinder.
But all you see are young pines,
every one a soldier.

The Aunt

As you would expect
she favored her own daughter,
and the name she'd call me
in that other language
she said with no malice
but impatience, somehow
quick and irritable—*krasavitza*.
I knew it meant clumsy,
but we were tough. After school
I'd go back to her house
and play with my cousin; she
knows all the words,
even that word, which meant beautiful.

Thomas and the Apostles

For the same reason
he was a carpenter
he stood there,
the others saying
it was true.
O but he must not count on this.

—If the Lord lives
let Him come to me,
even me, Thomas:
where in each place
there was a nail
I'd press my hand, print
where the nail slammed in.

Will they be broken,
those who are not supple?
last to believe
although they love no less.

Indian Graveyard

The willow makes grief visible.
On paper you know this—
a whole graveyard
encompassed by one tree bent
over a pile of broken clam shells
and the two gray tombstones,
almost all the sun
caught in the branches.
Do Indians have tombstones?
No, but otherwise
you think I couldn't tell.
You make your drawing
as sad as possible.

Circus

Often they seem to be falling forward
but I pretend not to notice
how well they use their bodies:
the girl, that tall delicate boy,
even the father in pink satin—
ardent, flashy. Now something scares me
and I turn away.

          In the dream
they walk the beach—
my children and their father—
equally exposed, ridiculous suits
in the same ice-cream colors.

Grave Goods

Dear wife, this is not An-yang:
we no longer believe in human sacrifice.
No need therefore to blind the two horses,
dig channels for the chariot wheels,
or quiet the frightened driver.
You will not be using a chariot
in the life that comes after.

But you will have your set of pitch pipes
and in simple jars your store
of dried fish and peaches,
beans and red ginger;
also, the mirror with the bronze back
and the little models of our life together—
a small clay house,
a small clay son and daughter.

Chrysalis

Inside, far inside,
the most beautiful paper
is unfolding.

Ivory edged in black,
a few blots
on the living skin.

Hinged wings
back to back,
most beautiful

and not for our pleasure.

Summer Night

Along the terrace railing
small unromantic flowers
open in all directions
and the wind moves on
to the white cloth, touches
its sharp creases, the two napkins,
an assembly of crystal.
Two people have just left the table
and it eludes you
why all of this should remain standing—
summer chairs, the empty pitchers,
the upright glasses—
until you see the gloves
next to a dish of berries
and the unfinished glass of brandy,
and then what baffles you, what hurts you most
is the impatience of the absent lovers.

The Daughters of Edward Boit

(after Sargent)

Paris, eighteen eighty-two.
The spaces between people are immense.
Two outsize Chinese vases in the hall
mark off the entrance to the drawing room.

Dressed, like her doll, in white,
Julia sits in the hallway on a pale green rug.
An older child, arms behind her back,
stands at the far left; her hair is red-gold
and her dress deep red. Whispers
behind the red screen in the corner.

                            The oldest girls
have stepped back toward the darkness.
White pinafores, black stockings,
like two Irish maids, they keep
close to the edges of the drawing room.
Jane stares out at the invisible easel;
the one who doesn't care is Flor,
slouching in profile on a Chinese vase.
She is thinking of the great spaces,
even between sisters.

Paris, eighteen eighty-two.
Three of you are looking straight ahead
as if nothing will ever happen outside this room.

Report from the Village

Terrible things are happening in slow motion:
a child turns in a low drifting fall,
a man finds cover in a doorway
where inside his shop the pharmacist
slumps over scales on the counter,
and a girl—bright skirt, hair flying—
tries to run, tries to scream.

Then in the street people
are quiet and figures swinging
from the terraces are quiet
and she is trying to open her mouth
as the officer from the mountains explains:

We did not massacre anyone.
We just surrounded the town
and did not let anyone surrender.

Polished Fragment

In the Eighteenth Dynasty
in yellow jasper
a queen impersonates a goddess.

Now behind glass
there is only her lower face—
unimaginable eyes
and the brow
gone completely, a Sahara
in deep shadow,
steep and cut away.
Everything finished comes to this.

So how extraordinary
that the mouth and chin
and the broken stalk of her neck
should be this beautiful
and we so subject
to beauty, prey to it,
desiring the curved mouth
that asks one-tenth of everything.

Green Fields of France

for *Harry*

Once when we were in Bruges
he insisted on renting a car and by himself
drove to Ypres and Polygon Wood.
And there were other forests, he said—
Sanctuary Wood, Hill 62—

In Normandy there were villages
with too many old women
and on some farms, under the grass,
the lines of trenches still visible;
and at the cemetery
on a mild afternoon he stood
helpless among the white crosses
as if to say
        I'm sorry.
I missed the Great War.
I was born in thirty-one,
even too young for the second.

If he could,
he'd apologize to every pilot
who ever kept a journal.

Yet what sends him hunting
for Omaha Beach, wrecked Spitfires,
the first lines of the British,
is not pity, but the occasion for courage.
He would give up anything
to have this chance,
to spiral down from the sky, RAF-style,
still believing in the enemy.

II

The Face of the Enemy

It was clear in my mind,
the consequences.
—Vidkun Quisling, 1945

I. Prelude

Berlin, December 1939

The King's name is never mentioned.
You explain the English danger,
their eyes on the iron mines,
blockades at Kristiansand, Stavanger—
possibly you exaggerate.

Hitler stares at the exquisite carpet,
promises funds,
but he can't intervene.

Major Quisling,
Norway is a neutral country.

19

II.   The Open Sea

All the way to Denmark
you leaned by the rail, watched
the bluish ice melting, melting.
The Germans sent Pieckenbrock
with his casual humiliating questions
about inlets and harbors—
if there is a plan,
he tells you nothing.

Then Tuesday, German troops inside the city,
banks closing—no King, no parliament—
this chance:
the same evening you broadcast your appointment.
As Prime Minister, you know you can save them,
but the people will not follow. Five days
and Norway is a German province,
and you never ask,
Is to stay to collaborate?

III.   Afternoons

On the dark afternoons
your secretary bends over his desk
scribbling in a small notebook.
And on all sides complicity.
After two years the Germans
came to their senses, named you
Minister President—
but the rioting hasn't stopped,
the schoolteachers choose
arrest, the ironworkers
still flaunt their insulting placards.
And the night at the university
when the students torched a building
you refused to go near the place,
so the Gestapo moved in.
Quick summers,
birds shrill in the branches
and something all wrong
as though the grass were poisoned.

IV.   Tribunal

Oslo, September 1945

Where were you the morning of the spring invasion?

Sleeping.

You insist you were uninformed?
Still, to invite the invader,
to stay when our King fled—
"Minister President," these
were crimes.

We were flying the Norwegian flag.
The guard was marching.

Which guard?

The King's. I was urging that we form
a government with the King. Then peace—

You are always talking about peace.
Would you describe it as peace,
the German ultimatum of April 9th?

We could have reached better terms.

Reply yes or no. If on April 9th
the government had agreed, would that
have meant peace?

Yes. But we might have reached better terms.

Yes. We have heard that before.

V. The Firing Squad

Akershus Fortress, Oslo
October 24, 1945

Notice the photographer.
He does not run forward.
No one comes. The pale boys
wait in their broken circle.
You know you'll fall
straight toward the heart of God—

quisling, you goose, you fool,
confusing your enemies,
mistaken in everything.

You became an embarrassment,
someone they can't let go,
someone they can't explain—
like the child of an enemy.
They can never forgive you.

III

Moira

It is me the moon follows—
as we drive I keep thinking
Could I leave you, or is this destined.
What if there are fates?
There might be three sisters,
it is possible; then each
has her errand, and the smallest,
holding scissors, is Atropos,
she who cannot be turned.
If we believe this, all we forfeit
trails us like a moon,
an appointment.

There might be three sisters
or just one woman.
After I loved
I took no risk.

Liebeslieder Walzer

I

She leans far back
as if she meant to dance
only with him—as if
they were testing how far she could bend
and not fall.
Past the small tables
a quartet singing,
a line of candles.
Now in a circle
embracing couples turn.
Even the host and his wife
dance as if the house
were not theirs;
and the song they asked for
tells of happiness, despair—
how they alternate
in a lover's heart.

II

People in pairs,
people in fine clothes—
with their singing
they will shut me out.
Someone grips my waist.
We pass the yellow candles,
chairs with their oval backs
turned toward the garden.

Outside the wind racing
and the stars blown, out of reach.
I ask what it means,
this dance in the dark,
and he smiles,
Nothing but what you see.

III

Surrender and possession
make one shape:
long limbs and no faces.
Did I ever dance
without thinking
the turns are to pursue,
to be desired,
and the lure, happiness.

IV

You came here with people
you have forgotten.
Like the songs, they have
nothing to do with dances.
All unimportant.

Concentrate on the young men
in black, the woman
with bared shoulders—
what you feared,
what you envy them,
is intensity.

Song of Past Feelings

This extravagance,
this giving in to sorrow,
I hate in you—

dangerous, the way the willow
seeking everywhere the same monotonous source
easily strangles
a house, another tree,
whatever blocks its path.

It is too difficult to love you
and yet to give up
at the moment I understand this
is heartless—
Who can shelter you?

The Persian

Trees, fountains, flowers,
and at the end, after all that blue,
he weaves in one row the wrong color—
as though in that perfect garden
he could just run out of blue.

Sly, like my mother.
A black thread tied to her carriage
insists there's nothing beautiful inside,
nothing so perfect
the eye might want it.

Marked by this, marked by this—
always her fear reminds me of some flaw.
Bare to the waist,
afraid to take a lover, I look
but at the mirror find nothing disfiguring.

What a long thread pulls
from child to mother.

View Downward

I

The main street in this village is a river.
It divides the town:
one half's on fire
and on the burning side
the houses are all pink.
Pink bridges are collapsing.
It's impossible to tell
who might be left behind.
And there is something
she wanted to tell him
but she can't remember.

After, we talk about the ending,
what she was trying to tell him.
You say it's that she loves him,
she has forgotten to tell him
she loves him. Why do men
always think that? She might
be asking for help,
I can't remember,
but it's not that, not
I love you.
It's something heartbreaking.

II

You are asleep—
Behind you is the house, white, empty,
and you stand in a field.
Why don't you move?
Everywhere there are
black and white roses
blowing. If you wanted
you could have them all.

What happens in your dream,
the dream of marriage?
You don't remember,
so it must be mine, and yours,
yours is the other dream:
a field of ice
and then the one flower, scarlet.

I think I know nothing about you.

III

Always I see myself
the one who wounds
and people would be angry,
they would think
The woman is unfeeling.

One day she decides
not to be touched.

Then he is far away, a dot,
and the woman I became
can only unravel her cruelty.
She is ashamed not to love him.

IV

There is a Russian trick:
a woman looks into a bowl of water
and tells your future.
But could she see the past?
I want to ask
what happened to us,
alone, in that unreal house,
with children
who grow passionate.

Driving back from the beach this September
we passed an inn
closed for the season.
At night I see the place—
a great square house, all white,
and outside on the long deserted terrace
four perfect white umbrellas.

V

The table is a circle of marble
and above us a wide umbrella spreads
its green stripes, illusions of protection.

Late afternoon and still
not everything is promised.

I wish that it were wartime,
both of us in danger:
I am the imagined woman,
the hero is waiting
and she comes to him—urgent, headlong.

But danger now comes
from the harsh interior.
You should be more afraid
of the long calm
unimaginable season
toward which this current takes us.

The Offer

Late summer. Flowers crowding in,
too many to be gathered. At night
an insistent hum, the moths frantic;
this morning, spiders tying
rose to rose. On her walk
she notes the way they have of falling
and the crushed ones, how they lie
pressed to the ground. Right now
she longs for iris, pale
heads on narrow stalks, translucent
filaments, lime trees in flower;
remembers early in the marriage
the hard things asked
and that she could not give them —
too late to come to him
asking for flowers.

Plain Song

Why long ago the Greeks wore
blue for deep mourning
I have no way of knowing.
Was it to blind themselves
with surface, iridescence;
or did they long for depth,
the deep bend from the waist,
the plunge,
and underneath
a slow uncoiling?
Whatever they wanted
was not ordinary:
each one, each one wore
something darker,
more brilliant.
Why they should choose
this for mourning
I have no idea,
but I know the blue—
and just as much I wanted
that strong isolating blue,
this dress and nothing else.
But not for grief. For love.

IV

The Delphians

What could go wrong under the Greek sun—
their bodies equal with the gods.
Down there the sheep are bleached stones.
An eagle's shadow burns into the cliff.
When they killed Aesop
they tossed him from the top,
watched him fall, cloak flapping.
Apollo's parasites he called them once.
And he was old by then:
everyone hates a moralist.
The beasts know who they are.

House at Stavanger

The architect is Irish:
for a friend in Norway he crosses the design
of Palladio's villa at Caldogno,
near Padua, with the plan
of a large Norwegian manorhouse.
He chooses the floors, gray-mauve,
the color of spruce trees;
doorknobs of solid brass;
coved ceilings, carved by hand,
one larch green (the boys' bedroom),
another claret, and in the music room—
bronze, gold, silver
feathers painted like Italian paper.

Country house for a friend,
dreamed gift. Their first day,
they are almost at dinner,
the boys upstairs, she cooking,
and the man setting up the table
in the old way as over and over
the sound of a Messerschmitt breaks through,
the doorway fills with fire.

> [*Stavanger—occupied April 9, 1940,*
> *the first day of the spring invasion*]

Coffee Trees

There were such fine blossoms,
almost too many,
but the yield
is not what I expected.
If I fail,
if I fail in this
I will come home.
We are planting shade trees.
No rain tonight, but the rows
are especially fragrant.
The moon is rising from behind the coffee.

Beggarman

A cane swings through the street
announcing him. He chooses something bent,
disfiguring—that branch
cut from a blackthorn tree
is polished and well made.
He dares you pity him.

Blackthorn, blackthorn,
have I become someone
who needs a crooked stick?

The Idea of North

Glenn Gould [1932–1982]

Someone is coughing so you hum a little.
Low as a child's chair, the piano stool
makes you even more ridiculous.
A virtuoso of the concert stage
turns to his audience. You tried.
You cannot present yourself.
When you look down, your hands
are over water. They must never
tire—as the sole rower
must not tire, must not
stare at the sun. Each turn
seen now from a boy's height,
cliffs so close and steep
you catch your breath,
then accelerate.

You call it North—
the glittering reclusive silence,
this music suddenly continuous.

Alexander III Bridge

Which Alexander were you—
the very cruel tsar,
the young man
who couldn't stop bleeding?
Passing under this bridge
we notice only the golden faces
set on an arch of steel—they must be gods,
gods of the river—
and above, like rows of torches, iron bridge lamps;
the globes have a violet tint.
And between these lamps we can almost
make out figures looking down on us—
women with impossible hats,
tall attentive men,
and one especially happy woman has no hat,
just a long cape and a feather boa.

And now we've passed it, we're passing
under another bridge and another,
Bridge of the Carrousel, New Bridge, Bridge
of the Money Changers, Saint Louis, Austerlitz,
until we've crossed all Paris
with its thirty-three bridges.

Daughter

Midwinter. Snow feathers the sky.
Paths disappear. Well water freezes.
The queen wishes for a daughter
white as snow . . .
                    You know the rest
before we've read the story:
the first queen dead in childbirth,
the mirror talking truth.
Composed, age four, hands folded on your lap,
you wait the offer of the poisoned apple.

Do not ask me to explain the second queen
shriveling with envy or the girl's
long sleep in her crystal coffin
and how at the end her eyes will open.
Patience. As in all fairy tales
it will be the child who prospers,
the parent who comes to a bad end.

Captain Thornton

Don't do this I tell myself,
and I won't. I won't
talk to the man my age,
khaki shirt, sleeves
rolled to the elbow.
He's black, he looks
like you might now.
It's summer. I want
to put my arm on the marble counter,
cold, against his arm—
just see what it looks like.

That's a lie, Captain Thornton.
The man looks nothing like you
and I do it often, thinking
No one is hurt by this.
               You were a boy,
I sent you away. But strangers,
why are they afraid of me—
white woman, woman of no importance.

The Balcony

The house in which you were not happy
is denied you: other people live there.
And still you want it back,
you keep thinking
now in that house it would be different—
insular, without argument,
asking less. You would plan
careful dinners and take walks
to the river. Like Wang Wei,
who could never decide
if he was a painter or a poet:
after his wife died he bought a house by a river
and from the red balcony under the ash trees
wrote each day to his friend
on the other side of the mountain.

The Hand

On the thirtieth day the hand is defined.
Classical, perfect,
a blueprint of the mother's.

The little bones,
set just so,
follow obedient

through the long months,
the fingers lengthening
in proper time.

But his is not a hand we recognize:
three perfect fingers
on a shortened arm.

Five is the golden number
in this scheme,
and terror deforms us all.

Invitation

You asked me to come
but I was afraid to leave the city—
the poets, none of whom I knew,
the hospitals (I might die),
and the news of other cities.

Over and over I read your letter:
*Dear love, here the trees bend
almost to the water—*
You walk the tall grass
waiting for an answer.

How do I enter this landscape?

The Spell

Remember taking root—
thighs stiffening,
arms branching out,
only the hair still moving.

Now movement frightens you most,
and the voice, suddenly
to have a voice.
This is the end of your enchantment.

It doesn't matter—
all the weight you carried.
Whatever is uprooted by your change
finds shelter elsewhere.

Long Illness

for Charlotte

Color is for children.
You will give it up—

Green earth, cobalt, rose madder

Slowly you wipe your brushes clean,
turn all your paintings
toward the wall, like faces.
And you experiment
in liquid plastic clear as glass,
use canvas, the background all sand—
I can't tell you, you said,
what one throws away—
try to live in a range of illness
without hope;
drink some poison,
come back, rest,
paint some more:

not much time,
the colors burning down
lampblack to ivory black.

Proof

for my daughter

On top the new globe
has a disc, half-moon and sun,
so when it's sunrise here
in Asia it is evening.
You slide your hand
across the black Atlantic.
India is red. Colors—
you wonder how they chose them.
It's beautiful,
but not what you wanted.

Why should I say
be satisfied.
I was like you—
vivid,
demanding proof—

you want a map
where you can touch the mountains.

Heaving In Coals by Moonlight

> *. . . tell him that indistinctness*
> *is my forte.*
> —J. M. W. Turner

At the edges flares
and at the center hollow,
a tunnel of moonlight
through which nothing passes.
All night he watches barges
up the Tyne: extended calm,
and deep in moored ships
men in gilded clusters
stoking coal. In the same sky
he puts the moon and sun.
It is a yellow morning.
Excessive. Like the dreams
of sudden ruin, complete disaster;
like everything he did. London critics said
the family was common (a barber's son)—
and as for coalmen,
why had he taken them as subjects,
wasting the moonlight?
But there are ways to want things
and who's to say
what we want is excessive.

Reply in the Dark

Sappho, who does not lie alone?
I fear this dangling sword,
the moon, and in the trees
an army of stars advancing.

Night Ferry

What made the beautiful one afraid to marry,
the shrewd one gamble everything?
Too late to ask about your sisters
or what it was like, your city.

This spring the orange trees mean nothing to you
and only your brothers and sisters
remember Black Sea Street.
                              But they are tired.
Chalk figures, thin with disappointment,
soon they will have vanished.
The ferry waits, and all of you are running.

I see you now, cast into furious sleep.
All the terrible things have happened
and tonight there is only a woman in a shawl
who paces the deck. Her back turned
to the Turkish coast, she watches
cities in motion, watches her sleeping children,
and the summer palace blazing in the water.

POETRY FROM ILLINOIS

History Is Your Own Heartbeat
Michael S. Harper (1971)

The Foreclosure
Richard Emil Braun (1972)

The Scrawny Sonnets and
Other Narratives
Robert Bagg (1973)

The Creation Frame
Phyllis Thompson (1973)

To All Appearances: Poems New
and Selected
Josephine Miles (1974)

Nightmare Begins Responsibility
Michael S. Harper (1975)

The Black Hawk Songs
Michael Borich (1975)

The Wichita Poems
Michael Van Walleghen (1975)

Cumberland Station
Dave Smith (1977)

Tracking
Virginia R. Terris (1977)

Poems of the Two Worlds
Frederick Morgan (1977)

Images of Kin: New and
Selected Poems
Michael S. Harper (1977)

On Earth as It Is
Dan Masterson (1978)

Riversongs
Michael Anania (1978)

Goshawk, Antelope
Dave Smith (1979)

Death Mother and
Other Poems
Frederick Morgan (1979)

Local Men
James Whitehead (1979)

Coming to Terms
Josephine Miles (1979)

Searching the Drowned Man
Sydney Lea (1980)

With Akhmatova at the Black Gates
Stephen Berg (1981)

More Trouble with the Obvious
Michael Van Walleghen (1981)

Dream Flights
Dave Smith (1981)

The American Book of the Dead
Jim Barnes (1982)

Northbook
Frederick Morgan (1982)

The Floating Candles
Sydney Lea (1982)

Collected Poems, 1930-83
Josephine Miles (1983)

The River Painter
Emily Grosholz (1984)

The Passion of the Right-Angled Man
T. R. Hummer (1984)

Healing Song for the Inner Ear
Michael S. Harper (1984)

Dear John, Dear Coltrane
Michael S. Harper (1985)

Poems from the Sangamon
John Knoepfle (1985)

Eroding Witness
Nathaniel Mackey (1985)
National Poetry Series

The Ghosts of Who We Were
Phyllis Thompson (1986)

9/19/89

In It
Stephen Berg (1986)

Palladium
Alice Fulton (1986)
National Poetry Series

Moon in a Mason Jar
Robert Wrigley (1986)

Lower-Class Heresy
T. R. Hummer (1987)

Poems: New and Selected
Frederick Morgan (1987)

Cities in Motion
Sylvia Moss (1987)
National Poetry Series